A map from Lowfields to Biggerton

Look at this map.

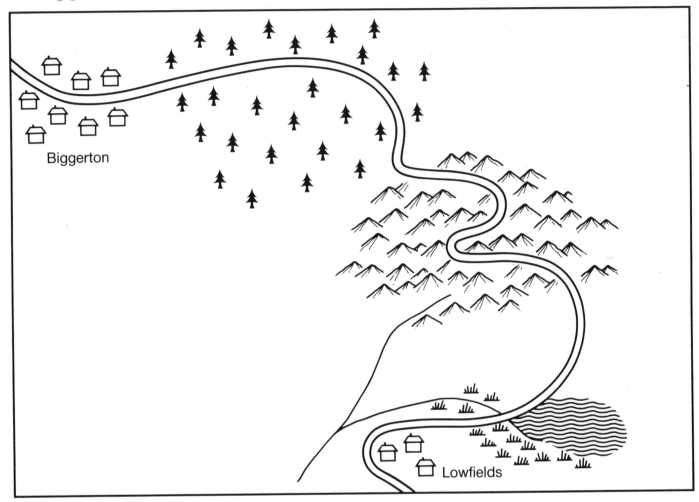

Mike Rowe is walking from Lowfields to Biggerton.

Look at these **signs**. (Another name for signs is **symbols**.)

Without the help of your teacher or friends, write down beside each sign what you think it might mean. You have **two** minutes.

Mike Rowe's journey

Below is a description of Mike Rowe's journey from Lowfields to Biggerton. Some of the words are missing.

Use the map to help you to fill in the missing words. Again, **do it on your own**. This time you have **five** minutes.

One sunny morning, Mike Rowe set off to walk from Lowfields to Biggerton. Not long after he started

out, the path went through a _____ Then it began to wind through _____

and the going was difficult and tiring. Mike had to rest.

Mike looked back at the way he had come. He could see the _____ which was very near his

home in Lowfields. He walked on. As he came to the other side of the _____ he could see,

over the tops of the _____, the smoke rising from the _____ of Biggerton.

If what you have written makes sense, it is correct.
- Now ask your neighbour if it makes sense to him/her.
- Does his/hers make sense to you? *Circle* YES/NO
- Have you both written **exactly** the same words? *Circle* YES/NO

You probably have not written the same words because the signs or symbols are not explained.

Every map needs an explanation of what its signs or symbols mean so that everyone can understand it.

The explanation of the signs on a map is called the **key**.

You need to use the key to help you understand what the map means.

A map with a key

You have already done an exercise where you had to work out the meaning of the symbols. If everyone in your class has not given the same meaning to each symbol, then the map has been understood in several different ways. So the map is no good. Therefore, **all maps should have a key** so that they are understood by everyone in the same way.

The map from Lowfields to Biggerton has been drawn again below. This time it has a **key**.

Using the map with the key, fill in the missing words in Mike Rowe's journey.

One sunny morning, Mike Rowe set off to walk from Lowfields to Biggerton. Not long after he started

out, the path went through a_____ Then it began to wind through_____

and the going was difficult and tiring. Mike had to rest.

Mike looked back at the way he had come. He could see the_____ which was very near his

home in Lowfields. He walked on. As he came to the other side of the_____he could see,

over the tops of the _____, the smoke rising from the_____ of Biggerton.

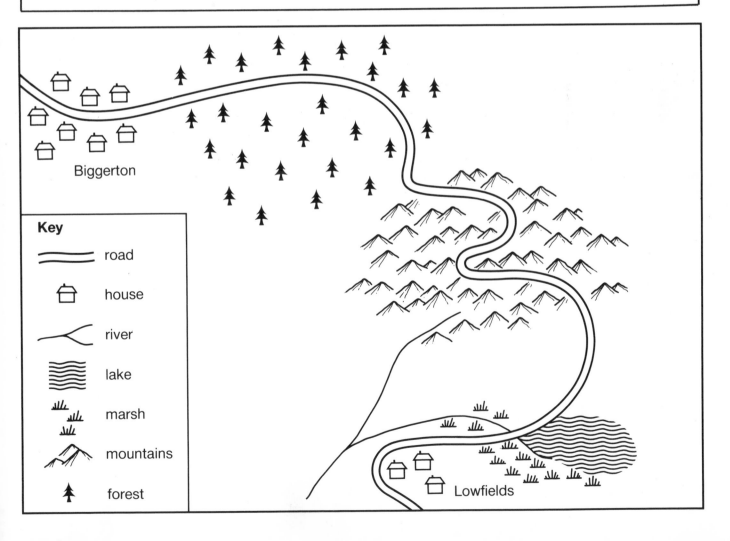

Biggerton

Key

road

house

river

lake

marsh

mountains

forest

Lowfields

A map of the town centre of Weston

On page 5 is a map of the town centre of Weston. The Balfour family live there at 10 Poplars Avenue.

Mr Balfour works at the Jobcentre.
Mrs Balfour does not do a paid job outside the home.
Susan goes to the junior school.
John goes to the playschool at St Mary's Church.

What to do

First, look at the map and find the places mentioned above. Then mark the following routes on your map.

● Draw a **blue** line to show which way Susan walks to the junior school with Mrs Balfour and John.

Mrs Balfour and John then walk from the junior school to the park to play for a while.

● Mark Mrs Balfour and John's route from the junior school to the park in **red**.

Mrs Balfour and John then go to the playschool at St Mary's Church.

● Mark their route from the park to the playschool in **green**.

Mrs Balfour leaves John at the playschool and goes shopping. She buys a magazine. Then she goes to the post office to collect some money. Last, she goes to the supermarket to buy some fish for tea.

● Mark Mrs Balfour's route from the playschool to the shops in **yellow**.

Mrs Balfour then takes the shortest route back to the playschool. She collects John and they walk home together.

● Mark their **shortest** route home in **black**.
● Complete the key below the map by filling in the correct colours for each of the routes.

A map of the town centre of Weston

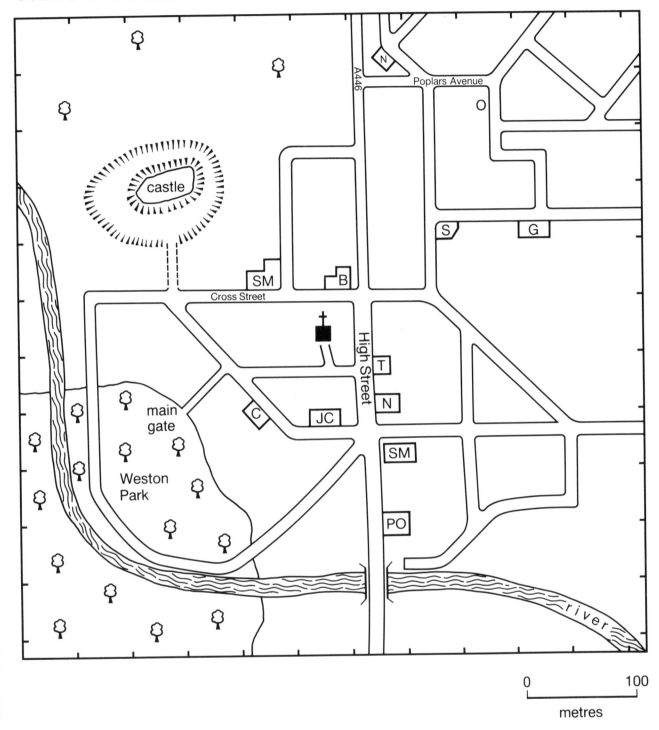

0   100

metres

Key to places on map

B   bank
C   coffee house   PO   post office
G   garage   S   junior school
JC   Jobcentre   SM   supermarket
N   newsagent   T   telephone
O   Balfours' home   ✝   St Mary's Church

Key to Mrs Balfour's routes

from home to junior school
from junior school to Weston Park
from Weston Park to playschool
from playschool to the shops
from the shops to home

Family Reunion

Look at the map of the world on page 7. On it are marked some cities, air routes, shipping lanes, railways and oceans.

Edna and Bruce Cobber are travelling from Australia to the United Kingdom to visit their relatives, the Pomeroys, in London.

1 Find Australia and the United Kingdom on the map.
2 Can the Cobbers go all the way by air?   *Circle*   YES/NO
3 Can they go all the way by sea?   *Circle*   YES/NO
4 Can they go all the way by rail?   *Circle*   YES/NO
5 How many air routes can they use?   *Circle*   1/3/5/6
6 How many ports would they call at if
  they were to travel all the way by sea?   *Circle*   1/3/5/6

As part of their trip, the Cobbers want to see the Golden Gate Bridge in San Francisco, Niagara Falls, the Statue of Liberty and the United Nations Building in New York. Edna has been unwell for some time and her doctor has recommended that she should start her holiday with a sea voyage. The Cobbers decide to visit San Francisco first.

7 Which ocean do they cross? _____

After enjoying San Francisco, they decide to go through the Rockies to Niagara Falls and New York.

8 How do they travel? _____

The Cobbers spend a long time in New York and suddenly realize that they have to get to London as quickly as possible.

9 Which ocean do they have to cross? _____

10 How should they travel across it? _____

After the reunion with the Pomeroys in London, the Cobbers visit Paris to see the Eiffel Tower. They then decide to go on to Moscow to see the Kremlin, and to Beijing (Peking) to see the Forbidden City and the Great Wall of China.

11 What would be their best means of travel from Paris to Beijing?

_____

12 How do they get from Beijing to Sydney?

_____

13 Next year, the Pomeroys will visit the Cobbers in Australia. Describe their shortest route from London.

_____

_____

The map for Family Reunion

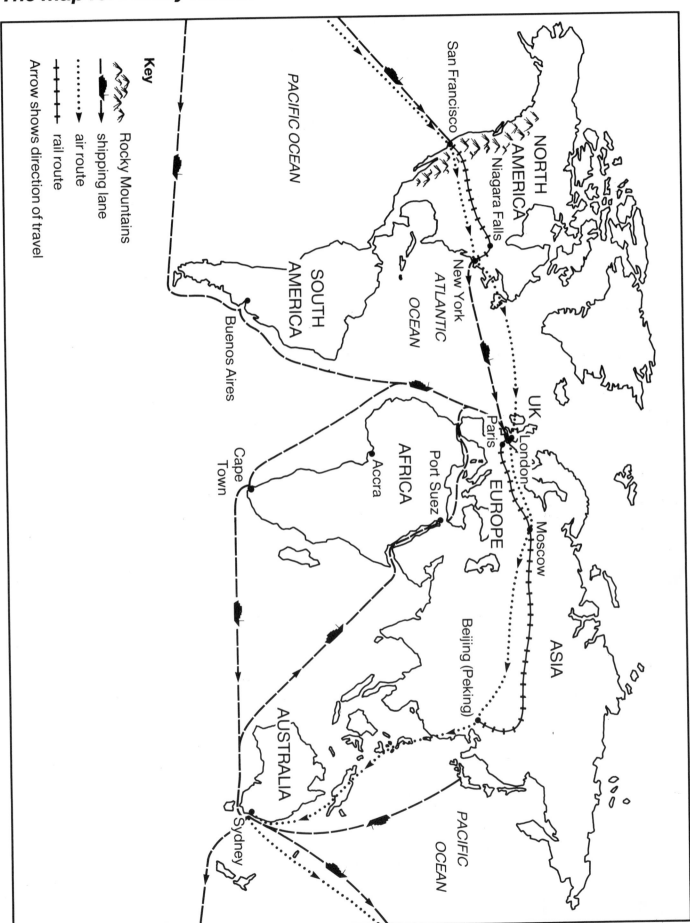

Name:

What is a grid?

A **grid** is made up of lines which are drawn across a map and lines which are drawn down the map, so that they divide the map into squares or rectangles. **Most maps have a grid.**

A grid helps you to find on the map the place you are looking for.

Ship-to-Port

This is a game you can play on your own.

In this game, you are the captain of a ship. Your ship springs a leak! You have to get your leaking ship to port as quickly as possible.

Below is a map showing the position of your ship and the position of the port. Your **ship** is in the square **Af**. The **port** is in the square **Fa**.

How to play

● On the map mark your route by drawing a ship symbol in each square you pass through to get to port. You should not need to go through more than **seven** squares to get to port.
● You can move your ship from square to square in any direction.
● Check the key of the map to make sure you know which is land and which is sea.

Key

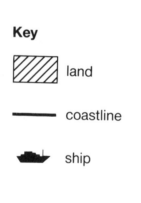

land

—— coastline

🚢 ship

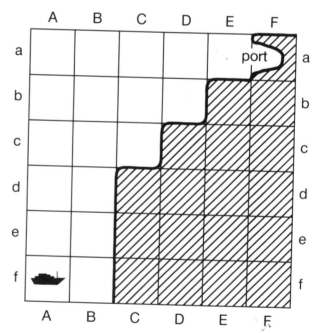

● When you have marked your route on the map, write down in the databank below the **two letters for each square** you have sailed through. These two letters are called the **grid reference** for their square. Remember to put the capital letter first.

Databank										
Move number	1	2	3	4	5	6	7	8	9	10
Square	Af									

A map with a grid

Some maps have a **lettered grid**, like the one in the game Ship-to-Port. Other maps use **letters and numbers**, like the one below.

Look at this map, then turn to page 10.

A map of Weston

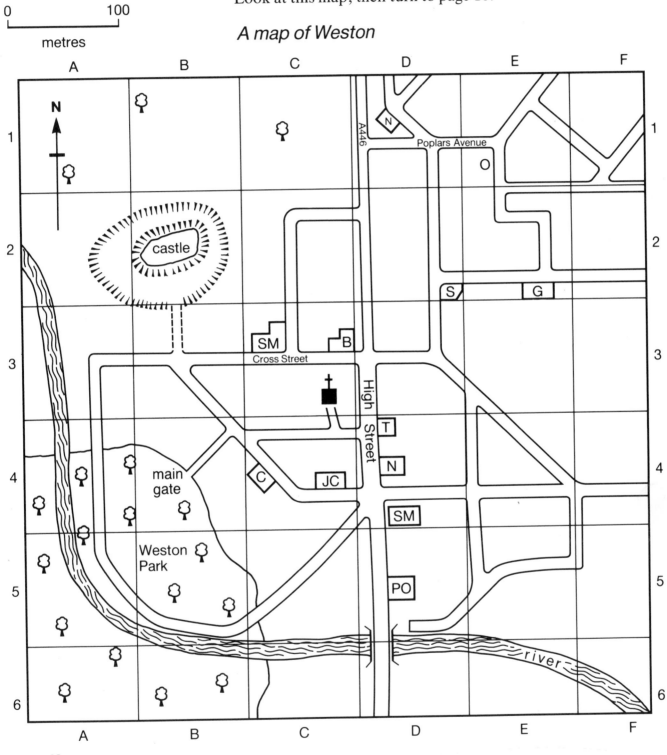

Key

B	bank	N	newsagent	SM	supermarket
C	coffee house	O	Balfours' home	T	telephone
G	garage	S	junior school	✝	St Mary's Church
JC	Jobcentre	PO	post office		

Some grid references

When you describe routes such as those Mrs Balfour took on page 4, it is helpful to give **grid references**. These show exactly where places are on the map.

The journeys made by Mrs Balfour and her children are described again below. This time spaces have been left (inside brackets). In these spaces, put in the grid reference of each place mentioned. The first grid reference has been done for you.

Mrs Balfour, John and Susan leave home and walk to Susan's school (D2). Mrs Balfour and John then walk from the school to the main gate of Weston Park (   ) to play for a while. Mrs Balfour and John then go to the playschool at St Mary's Church (   ). Mrs Balfour leaves John at the playschool and goes shopping. She buys a magazine at the newsagent (   ) and then goes to the post office (   ) to collect some money. Finally, she goes to the supermarket (   ) to buy some fish for tea. Mrs Balfour then takes the shortest route back to the playschool (   ). She collects John and they walk to their home in Poplars Avenue (   ).

The map index

Look at the map on page 9. You will see that Poplars Avenue, the Jobcentre, Weston Park, High Street, St Mary's Church and the junior school are all marked on the map.

What to do

● Arrange these places in alphabetical order on the lines below.
● Beside each place, write the correct **grid reference**. Put the letter before the number.

_____   _____

_____   _____

_____   _____

_____   _____

_____   _____

_____   _____

You have made a map index.

Most street maps have a map index. The index will help you to find any place on the map.

Name:

Stick-a-Map

Some map signs are drawn below. Each one is in a box.

What to do
- Colour in each sign using the colour given on the left of its box. If no colour is shown, **do not** colour in that sign.
- When you have finished colouring, cut out each box.
- Stick these boxes into the correct squares on the map on page 12. You can find the correct square by using the grid reference given on the right of each box. The first has been done for you. The map also has parts of a road and railway on it to help you.

colour		sign	ref	colour		sign	ref
brown		church	L4	red		railway station	I 2
		school	N5	black		factory	E12
		woods	H8	red		hospital	J10
black		crossroads	M2	blue		police station	K1
black		roundabout	M11	orange		airport	B10

Under the map on page 12 is a databank with some more signs. These signs are also drawn below in boxes.

- Colour in each sign using the colour given on the left of its box. If no colour is shown, **do not** colour in that sign.
- When you have finished colouring, cut out each box. Stick these boxes into any empty squares on the map on page 12.
- When you have put a box in a square, write the grid reference of the square in the databank below the map.

colour		sign	colour		sign
red		telephone	brown		castle
red		postbox	yellow		cafe
red		garage	blue		lake
green		farm	yellow		doctor
brown		public house	red		town hall

Name:

The map for Stick-a-Map

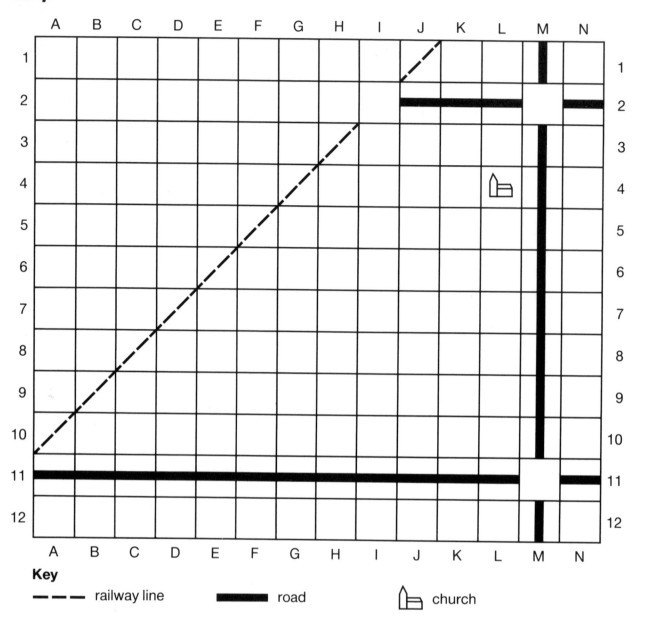

Key

--- railway line　　▬▬▬ road　　church

Databank				
Symbol	**Grid reference**	**Symbol**	**Grid reference**	

Don't forget to colour these signs also.

Grids with letters, or numbers and letters

In Ship-to-Port on page 8 and in the map of Weston on page 9, the squares were **lettered** or **numbered and lettered**. In the map for Build-a-Line on page 14, the lines are **numbered only**. They can be used as grid references in exactly the same way as the lines of latitude and longitude.

Build-a-Line

This is a game for two players.

The aim is to build a railway line between the bottom and top edges of the grid on the map on page 14. The winner is the first player to complete his/her own line.

How to play

● You will need a pack of playing cards. The numbered cards are 2 to 10. The Jack is 11. The Queen is 12. The King is 13. The Ace is 1.
● Take the pack of cards and divide it into **red** cards and **black** cards. You now have two packs.
● Shuffle each pack of cards separately and place them face down.
● The players take turns. The first player takes one card from each pack.
● The player looks at them and uses the two numbers they stand for to plot a point in the **middle** of a square on the grid. The number on the **black** card stands for the same number **across** the grid. The number on the **red** card stands for the same number **up** the grid.

Example
Cards drawn: 3 of hearts and 4 of spades

first player — red numbers

black numbers

second player

● The second player then draws a card from each pack and plots the numbers they stand for.
● **Note:** a player may only plot points on **his/her side** of the map. If the point is on the other player's side of the map, that turn does not count.
● A player can only join up points when they are in squares **next to each other**.
● Build the line in sections of **one** square at a time. The line should go from the **middle** of one square to the **middle** of the next square.

Example These points may be joined.

These points may **not** be joined until another point has been plotted between them.

● If the cards run out, reshuffle each pack and start again.

The grid for Build-a-Line

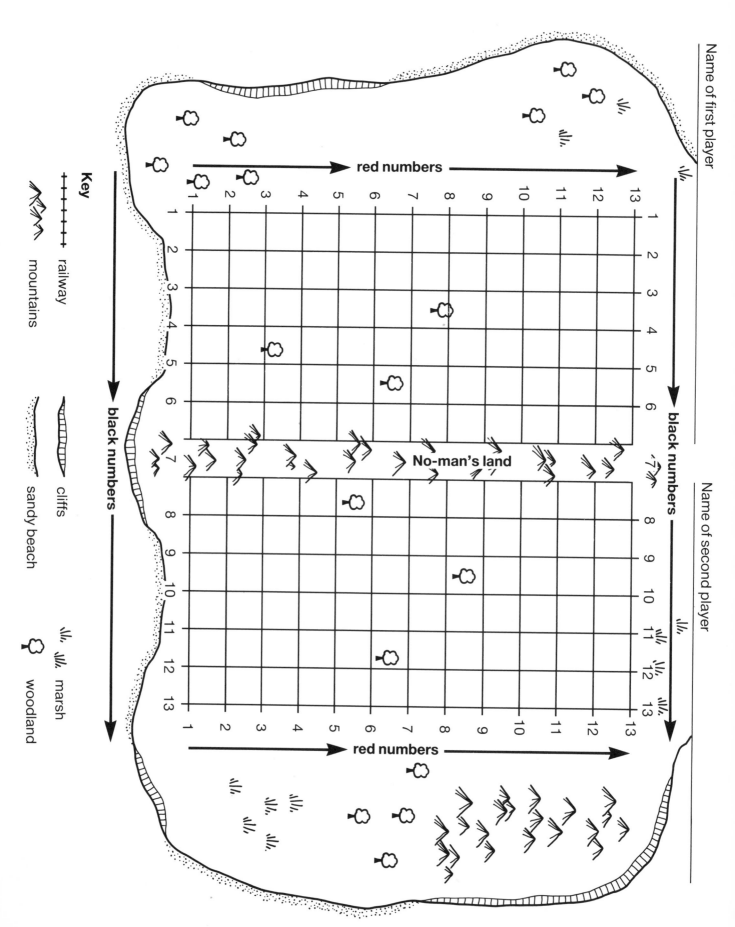

Rescue the Fell Walker

This is a game to play on your own.

A fell walker has got lost. She has also broken her leg and is lying helpless in square 0071. You are a police dog handler and you have five dogs.

How to play

● To find the walker and help rescue her, you have to surround her with the dogs. You must do this in as **few moves as possible.**
● You can move **in any direction.**
● In the **correct three squares** on the grid, draw and name the three dogs you will use to completely surround the injured fell walker.
● Now fill in the table below the grid.

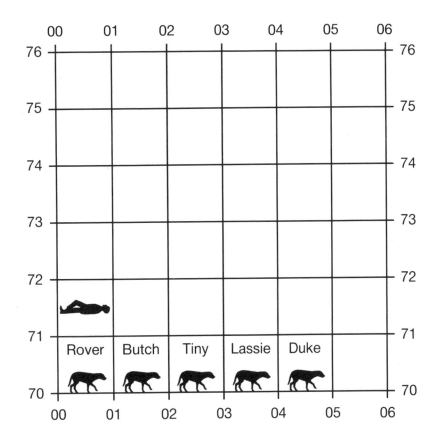

Record of moves		
Name of dog	**Last square moved to**	**Squares moved through to reach its final square**
Rover	0070	None
Butch	0170	None

Catch Ringo

This is a game for two players.

The Ringo Kid is a well-known bandit. He has robbed a bank and he is being chased by a posse. The posse has to surround the Ringo Kid so that he cannot move.

How to play

● One player is the Ringo Kid. Ringo starts in square 0273 on the grid below.
● The other player is the sheriff in charge of the posse. The starting position of each member of the posse is shown on the grid by the letter **P**. Each member of the posse has a number — 1, 2, 3, 4, 5 or 6.
● Each man on the map can be moved **one square** at a time. He can be moved in **any** direction. The move must be **written in the log** on page 17. **Carefully read the instructions on that page.**
● Ringo and the posse take turns to move. Only **one** posse member can move at a time. **Ringo** must move **first**.
● No one can be moved into a square which has already been used.
● Each player has 30 moves. If after 30 moves the Ringo Kid can still move, then he is the winner.

The grid for Catch Ringo

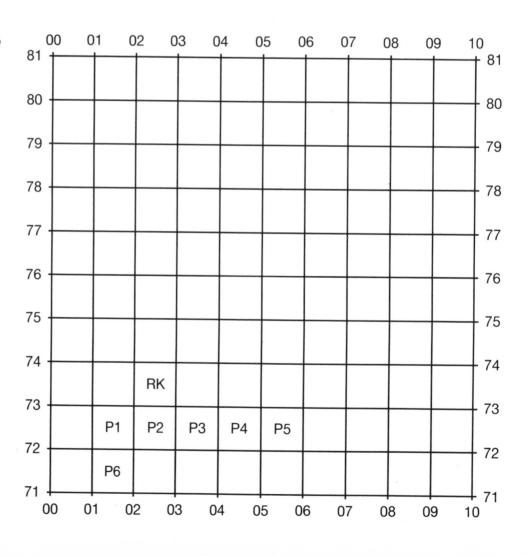

2. GRIDS

Name:

The log for Catch Ringo

- Record in this table **every move** made by each man.
- Write in the **grid reference** for each new square used. The starting positions are already written in.
- Any move wrongly recorded in the log puts that person out of the game.

Move	Ringo Kid	Posse members					
		1	**2**	**3**	**4**	**5**	**6**
Starting position	0273	0172	0272	0372	0472	0572	0171
1							
2							
3							
4							
5							
6							
7							
8							
9							
10							
11							
12							
13							
14							
15							
16							
17							
18							
19							
20							
21							
22							
23							
24							
25							
26							
27							
28							
29							
30							

Ringo's Last Stand

This is a game for two players.

In this game, the posse has caught up with the Ringo Kid. The players decide who is going to be Ringo and who is going to be the sheriff in charge of the posse of six.

How to play
- Each player needs a copy of the grid below.
- The player who is Ringo draws a picture of Ringo in **any one square** in the **top half** of the grid.
- The player who is sheriff draws a picture of each of the six posse members in **six squares** in the **bottom half** of the grid.
- The player who is Ringo also draws **five** large boulders in **five squares** in the **top half** of the grid. No boulder must be in the same square as Ringo, but **one** of these boulders must be in a **square next to Ringo.**
- The players must **not show** their grids to each other.
- Ringo fires the first shot by giving the grid reference of the square which he wants his shot to hit. The next shot is fired by the posse. Again, the grid reference of the target square is given. Then another shot is fired by Ringo, and so on.
- Each player must record his/her own shots on **his/her own grid.** Remember, all of Ringo's shots will hit squares in the posse's half of the grid and all of the posse's shots will hit squares in Ringo's half of the grid.
- When one player fires a shot, the other will say what the shot has hit. A shot can hit the Ringo Kid, a boulder, a posse member, or nothing.
- In order to win, Ringo must hit every member of the posse without being hit himself. If he is hit, the sheriff is the winner.

The grid for Ringo's Last Stand

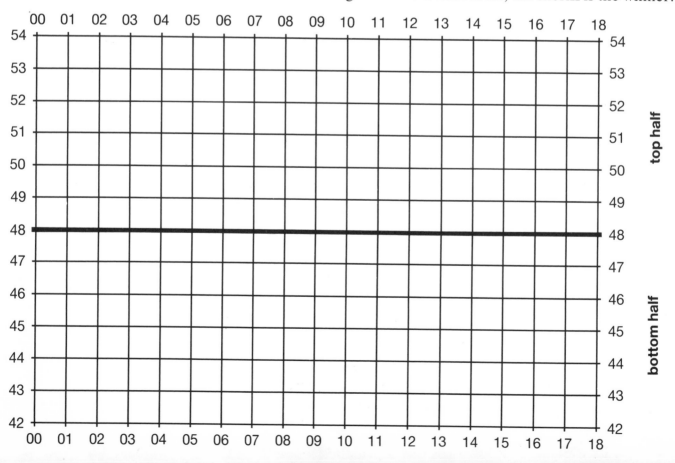

3. COMPASS DIRECTIONS   Name:

Compass directions

You can give the position of a place on a map by using grid references.

Another way of giving the position of a place on a map is to use **compass directions**. **North**, **south**, **east** and **west** are compass directions.

Imagine that a compass is placed at point A on the map below. The four directions of north, south, east and west are marked on the map.

A map of the world showing some compass directions

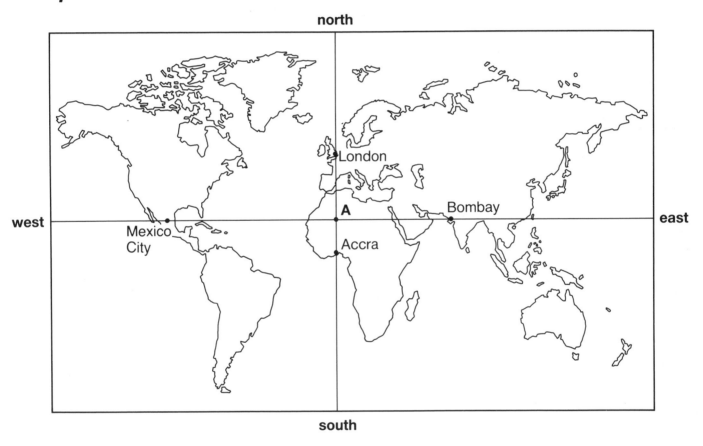

1 Is London **north** or **south** of point A? _____

2 Which city lies to the **west** of A? _____

3 Which city lies to the **east** of A? _____

4 Which city lies to the **south** of A? _____

5 What is the name of the continent where the compass has been placed? (You may use your atlas to answer this question.) _____

Compass directions from London

There are directions **between** north, south, east and west. They are **north-east**, **south-east**, **south-west** and **north-west**.

On this map of Great Britain, the centre of the compass is on London.

1 Name one place which is directly **north** of London.

_____

2 Name one place which is **north-east** of London.

_____

3 Name one place which is directly **east** of London.

_____

4 Name one place which is **south-east** of London.

_____

5 Name one place which is directly **south** of London.

_____

6 Name one place which is **south-west** of London.

_____

7 Name one place which is directly **west** of London.

_____

8 Name one place which is **north-west** of London.

_____

You have described the compass direction of eight places **from** London. A compass direction is given **from one place to another**.

● With the compass centred on London, Coventry is north-west **from** London. (Usually we would write or say 'north-west *of* London'.)

● With the compass centred on Coventry, London is south-east **from** Coventry. (Likewise, 'south-east *of* Coventry'.)

Compass directions from Coventry

On this map of Great Britain, the centre of the compass has been moved from London to Coventry. From London, the compass has moved to the
n_____ w_____ .

Again, eight compass directions are shown. They are north, south, east and west, and the four directions between them—north-east, south-east, south-west and north-west.

1 Name one place which is **north** of Coventry. _____

2 Name one place which is **north-east** of Coventry. _____

3 Name one place which is **east** of Coventry. _____

4 Name one place which is **south-east** of Coventry. _____

5 Name one place which is **south** of Coventry. _____

6 Name one place which is **south-west** of Coventry. _____

7 Name one place which is **west** of Coventry. _____

8 Name one place which is **north-west** of Coventry. _____

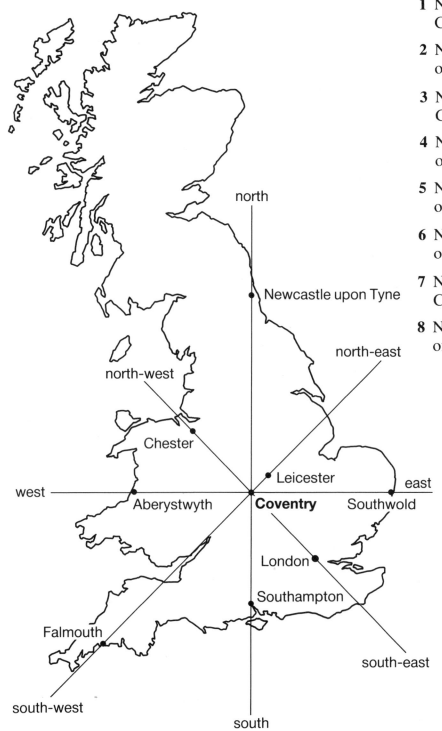

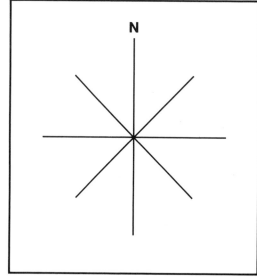

The star shape formed when the eight compass points are drawn together is called a **compass rose**.
Complete the labelling of the compass rose above.

Compass directions in Weston

Your teacher will give you a piece of tracing paper. Trace on it the compass rose from page 21.
- Put the centre of your compass rose on point **X** in square **D2** on the map below.
- Make sure that **north on the compass rose points straight to the top** of the map.

A map of Weston

Key

B	bank
C	coffee house
G	garage
JC	Jobcentre
N	newsagent
O	Balfours' home
PO	post office
S	junior school
SM	supermarket
T	telephone
✝	St Mary's Church
═	Balfours' walk

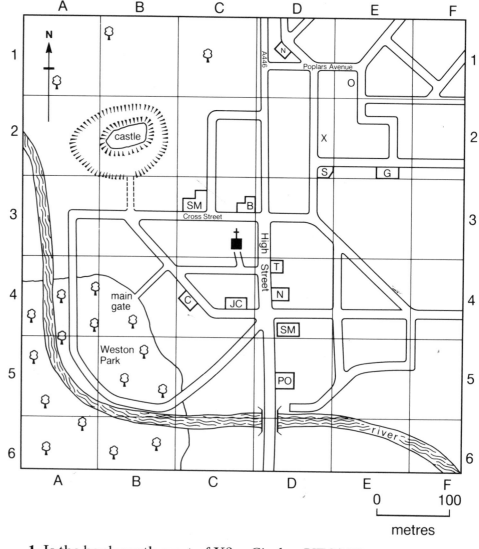

1 Is the bank south-west of X?   *Circle*   YES/NO
2 Is the school south of X?   *Circle*   YES/NO
3 Is the castle west of X?   *Circle*   YES/NO

- Now put the centre of your compass rose on St Mary's Church.
- Make sure that **north on the compass rose points straight to the top** of the map.

4 What is the direction of the castle from St Mary's Church? _____

5 What is the direction of the coffee house from the church? _____

6 What is the direction of the Jobcentre from the church? _____

7 What is the direction of point X from the church? _____

8 What is the direction of the newsgent (D4) from the church? _____

The Balfours go for a walk

The Balfour family goes for a walk in Weston taking this route:

▶ From their home in Poplars Avenue they walk **west**, past the crossroads and reach the main road, the A446.

▶ They turn **south** and walk towards the centre of the town.

▶ At the first road junction they turn **west** again and follow the road.

▶ After a short distance they turn **south** into Cross Street. At this point, they turn **west** and walk to the crossroads.

▶ At the crossroads they turn **north**.

What to do

● On the map on page 22, mark the route followed by the Balfours. Use a **green** pen or pencil.

● Complete the key to the map by colouring in the sign for the Balfours' walk.

● Which place have they visited? _____

A report of the Balfours' home journey is given in the big box below. There are some words missing. These words are in the small box below. Put them into the right spaces in the big box. Cross each one out as you use it. You will need to look at the map on page 22.

After leaving the _____ the Balfours walk back to the crossroads

on Cross Street. Here they turn _____ . They walk as far as the main

street in the town which is called _____ _____ . Here they

turn _____ and then _____ into Poplars Avenue. Their house is

on the _____ side of Poplars Avenue.

The missing words are
High Street, east, castle, south, east, north

Flight

Below is a map of the continents which lie beside the Atlantic Ocean. The continents are **Europe, Africa, South America** and **North America**.

● Label each continent by putting a name in the correct box on the map.

On the map is a compass rose. More compass directions have been added, making **16 directions**. You can see what these 16 directions are by looking at the key to the compass rose.

● Make a **careful tracing** of the compass rose.

From	→	To	Direction
London	→	Paris	SSE
Paris	→	A - - - -	
	→		
	→		
	→		
	→		
New York	→	London	

Starting from London, you are going to fly round clockwise to each of the cities shown. The direction **north** has been drawn above each city.

● Place the compass rose you have traced over each city in turn to find the direction in which you will have to travel to reach the next city. Now complete the box on the left. The first direction has been done for you.

● Remember to line up the **N** of the compass with the **N** above each city.

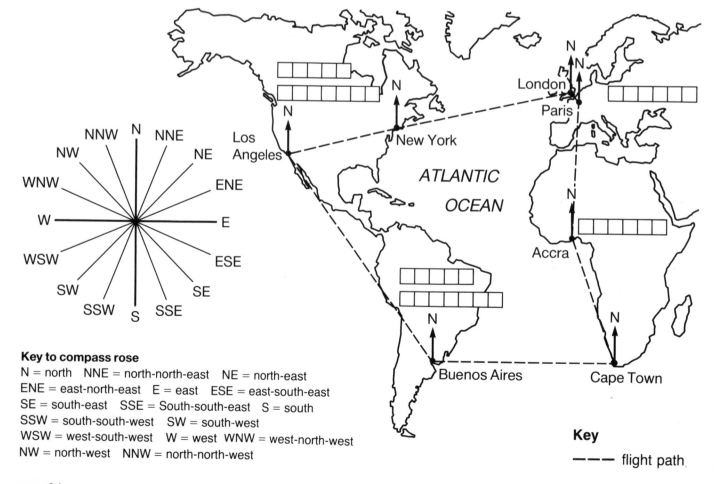

Key to compass rose
N = north   NNE = north-north-east   NE = north-east
ENE = east-north-east   E = east   ESE = east-south-east
SE = south-east   SSE = South-south-east   S = south
SSW = south-south-west   SW = south-west
WSW = west-south-west   W = west   WNW = west-north-west
NW = north-west   NNW = north-north-west

Key
- - - - flight path

Charter

This is a game for two players.

Each player owns a charter airline company. Each player's aircraft is to leave London and fly to ten cities. It then returns to London. The winner is the player who does this first.

The routes along which each player can fly are shown by the lines on the map on page 26.

How to play

● You will need a die and a different coloured pencil for each player.
● Take turns to throw the die.
● If a **1** is thrown, fly either **north** or **south**.
   If a **2** is thrown, fly either **north-east** or **north-west**.
   If a **3** is thrown, fly either **east** or **west**.
   If a **4** is thrown, fly either **south-east** or **south-west**.
   If a **5** is thrown, the aircraft has engine trouble. **Miss one turn.**
   If a **6** is thrown, you get a **free choice**. Fly in **any direction** you choose.
● If you take a wrong direction, your aircraft will crash and your opponent will be the winner.
● If you choose to **fly over** a city, you **cannot count it** in your total.
● Plot your route on the map on page 26 and complete the log on page 27. If you take more than 32 moves, ask your teacher for another log sheet.

The aircraft shown below are used by the world's big airlines. Fill in the names of these aircraft if you know them.

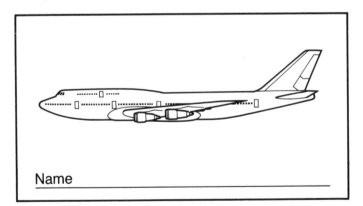

Name

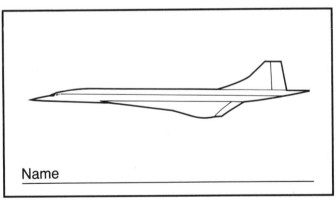

Name

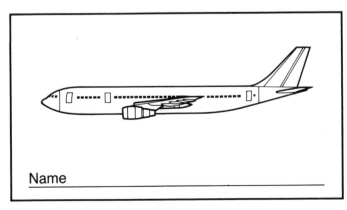

Name

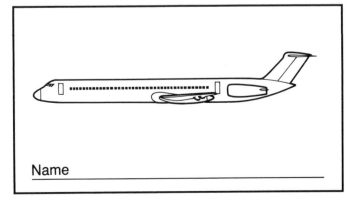

Name

The map for Charter

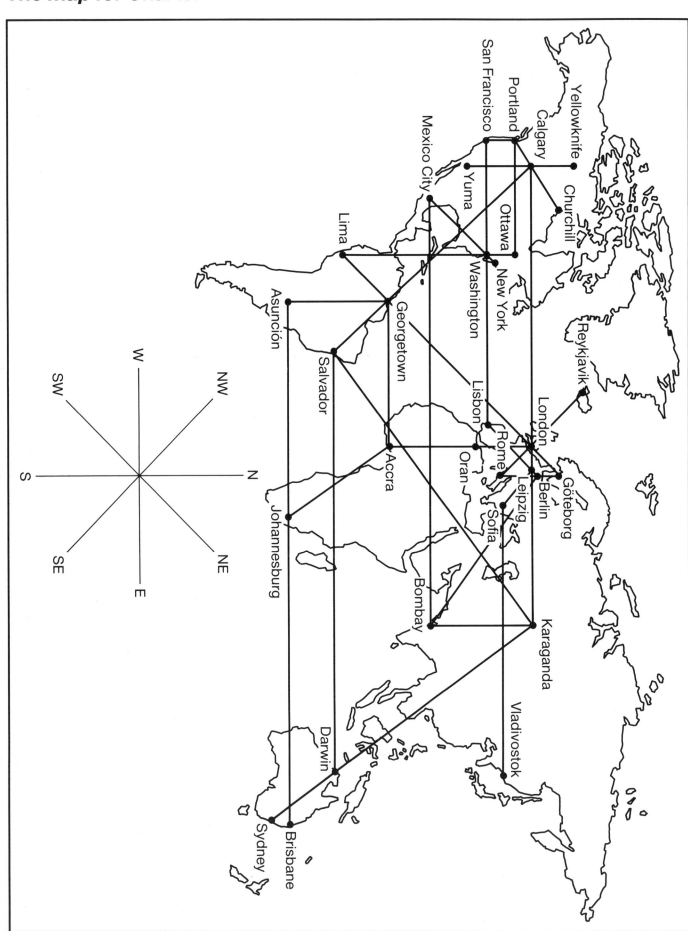

3. COMPASS DIRECTIONS

Name:

The route log for Charter

Your route

Start	London To →				
Throw no.	To	Tick if landing	Throw no.	To	Tick if landing
1			17		
2			18		
16			32		

Your opponent's route

Start	London To →				
Throw no.	To	Tick if landing	Throw no.	To	Tick if landing
1			17		
2			18		
16			32		

Treasure Hunt

A treasure chest is hidden on an island. The map of the island is on page 29.

Instructions 1 to 11 below tell you how to find the treasure. There are some words missing. The number of letters in each missing word is shown by the number of dashes.
- Fill in the missing words in the right places on the map and also in the crossword below.
- If you have filled in the crossword correctly, the letters in the column A will make the name of the pirate who buried the treasure. If you have the right answers then you have found the treasure!
- Mark your route on the map with a coloured pencil.

How to find the treasure chest

1 Land on the beach in Conky Cove (square E10).
2 Go **west** 3 km (3 squares) to square E7. Here you discover b – – – – of a skeleton. The skeleton's finger points **south**.
3 Walk 5 km to the River L – – (square J7).
4 Follow the river **south-west** to square K6. Here you stop and drink the milk from a – – – – – u –.
5 Now walk to square K12. You have walked e – – –.
6 Here, in square K12, pick a b – – – – –.
7 From this spot go to square H16. You have walked in a – – – – – e – – – direction.
8 Spend the night sheltering in the – a – – –.
9 Go **east** 2 km (to square H18). Here you find another skeleton hanging by a r – – –.
10 Go **north** to square E18. On the way you have to build a – – – d – – to cross a gorge.
11 Go **west** to square E14 where you will find the treasure.

Whose treasure is it? _____

Can you see your ship? _____

Crossword

The map for Treasure Hunt

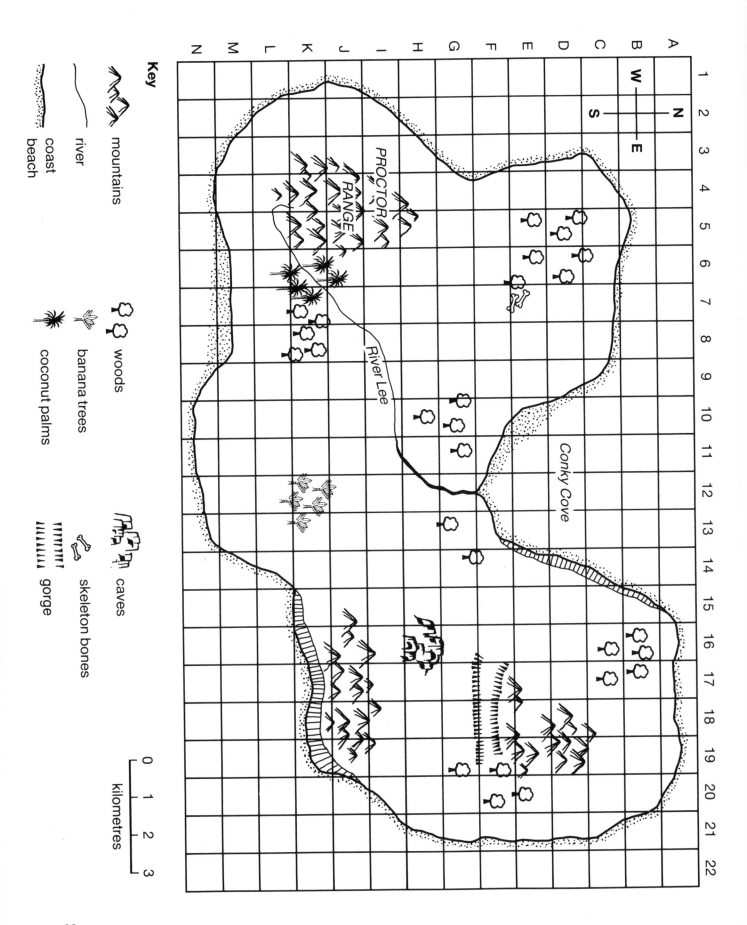

First to the Treasure

This is a game for two players.

Treasure is buried on an island, a map of which is on page 31.

Each player has a copy of this map and of the crossword on page 33.

The winner is the player who either reaches the treasure first by the correct route, or finds the password first by completing the crossword.

Each move must be marked on the map, or put in the crossword.

Do not let your opponent see your map or crossword.

How to play

● For each move toss a coin. The **map** is **heads** and the **crossword** is **tails**.
● When you throw **heads**, do what it says in the **heads column** on page 32. The heads column tells you what to do on the **map**.
● When you throw **tails**, answer the clues in the **tails column** on page 32. The tails column tells you what to write in the **crossword**.
● Carry out the instructions in the two columns in **strict order**. For example, if your first throw is heads, and then heads again for your second throw, do what it says beside 1 and 2 in the heads column by marking a route on the map. If your third throw is tails, then you must answer the clue beside 1 in the tails column, and write the answer in 1–across in the crossword. If your fourth throw is heads, you must do what it says beside 3 in the heads column, and mark your route on the map.

When you have reached the treasure by following the instructions in the heads column, the route you have drawn will resemble the shape of a continent. Which one?

_____

The map for First to the Treasure

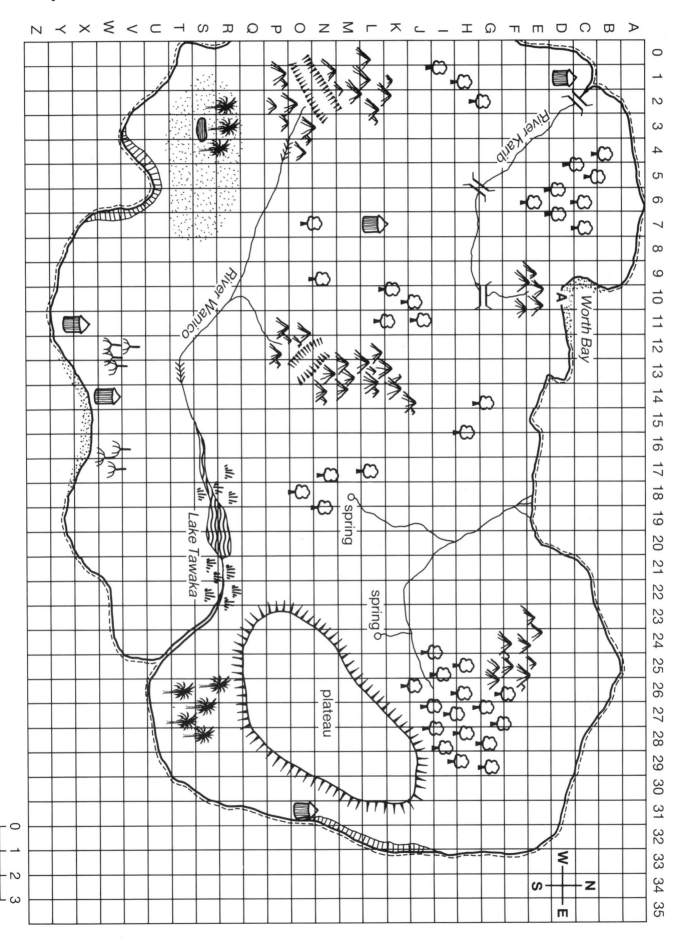

Name:

The heads and tails columns for First to the Treasure

Heads column (map)	Tick when completed	Tails column (crossword)	Tick when completed
Start at Worth Bay, point A			
1 Move south-west to the bridge over the River Karib.		1 Land next to the sea.	
2 Move directly south three full squares.		2 You are looking for this.	
3 Move to Tupi village at L7.		3 You will find these on the map in H27.	
4 Travel east to the foot of the mountains.		4 Where the river falls.	
5 Turn south for two squares.		5 You travelled across this to get to the island.	
6 Travel south-east through the gorge.		6 Their villages are on the island.	
7 At the end of the gorge, turn south again to the waterfall on the River Wanico.		7 Wanico is one.	
8 Cross the waterfall and walk to U14.		8 A very dry place.	
9 You are lost. Go to the fishing village directly south.		9 To be found in a very dry place.'	
10 The headman of the village guides you east through the mangrove swamps to W18.		10 Spr——.	
11 He tells you to go north-east to the swampy shores of Lake Tawaka (R21).		11 Found in square R20.	
12 Go north four full squares to N21.		12 You might be poisoned by these reptiles on the way to the treasure.	
13 Go north-east to the freshwater spring.		13 A sort of swamp.	
14 You will find the treasure where J meets three pieces of eight—north from the spring.		14 A precious metal.	

The crossword for
First to the Treasure

The key for
First to the Treasure

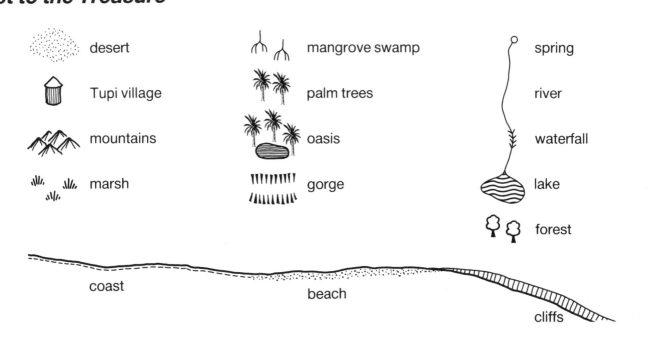

desert

Tupi village

mountains

marsh

mangrove swamp

palm trees

oasis

gorge

spring

river

waterfall

lake

forest

coast

beach

cliffs

The Grand Old Duke of York

Any number may play this game.

The winner is the player who finishes the nursery rhyme first. Before you start the game, make the spinner shown below left.

How to play

● Each player has a copy of the 'hill-and-valley' chart and the incomplete nursery rhyme (see below).
● Decide who goes first.
● Start at York with 10 000 men.
● March your men to the top of the hill by using the spinner to get the words **move to up**.
● When the spinner stops at **up**, draw a **red** line from York up to **1**, which is the top of the hill.
● When you have marched your men up to 1 (the top of the hill), fill in the rhyme on your own sheet with the word **top** next to 1. Use **red**.
● Keep spinning in turn until you get the words on the spinner which let you move on to points 2, 3, 4, 5, 6 and 7.
● At each point write the missing word in the space beside the number in the rhyme.

The spinner
Cut out the paper pattern, glue it to a piece of card and make a hole in the middle for a matchstick.

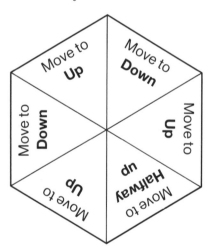

The Grand Old Duke of York
He had ten thousand men

He marched them up to the (1) _____ of the hill

And he marched them (2) _____ again.

And when they were (3) ___ they were (3) ___

And when they were (4) _____ they were (4) _____

And when they were only (5) _____

They were neither (6) ___ nor (7) _____

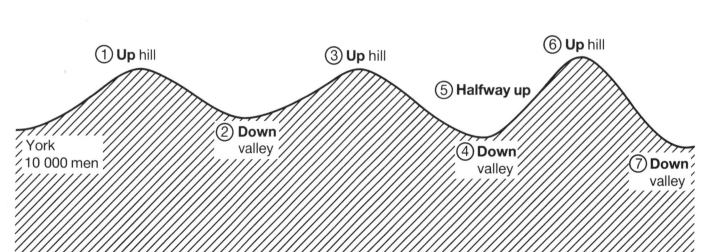

Delivery

This is a game for two or three players.

The aim is to deliver a newspaper to four places and end up at the disco. The places are marked **D** on the chart below. The winner is the first player to arrive at the disco.

How to play

● You need one pack of playing cards and two or three different coloured pencils.
● Divide the pack into **red** cards and **black** cards. You will then have two packs – a pack of red cards and a pack of black cards.
   The **black** cards allow you to move **from left to right** along the road.
   The **red** cards allow you to move **into and up and down** the buildings.
   The **picture** cards **do not allow you to move** at all.
   The Ace counts as 1.
● Use the coloured pencil to mark your progress.
● Decide who goes first.
● In turn, start by taking a card from the **black** pack. You need to get to square 4 so that you can deliver your first newspaper.

● The number on the **black** card which you take tells you how many squares you may move. If your first card is 4 or smaller than 4, you can move according to that number. For example, if you take a 2 of spades, move to square 2. If it is a 3 of clubs, move to square 3.
● If you take a black card whose value is **higher** than the number you need, you **cannot move**.
● When you land on squares 4, 10, 21/22/23 and 30/31, take a **red** card. Then move up to the bungalow, house or flat to make your delivery. Only a **red Ace** will allow you to make a delivery to the **bungalow**.
● When you have made your delivery, you must come down to the road again by taking **red** cards.
● You may then take a **black** card and move along towards the next place. You will then take a **red** card to make the delivery.
● When you have used up a pack, shuffle it and use it again.
● You must get the **right number** to land on the square needed.
● You will need a **red Ace** to get into the disco at the end.

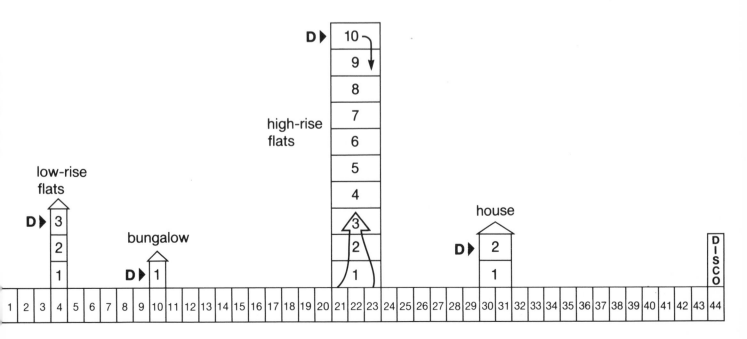

Make a model

The shape drawn here shows a number of heights.

● Colour each section as follows.

Between 0 and 10 m	**light green**
Between 10 and 20 m	**dark green**
Between 20 and 30 m	**orange**
Between 30 and 40 m	**light brown**
Between 40 and 50 m	**dark brown**
Above 50 m	**purple**

● Cut out the whole shape. Fold it around. Then fix flap **A** under the other side of the shape where shown by the arrow.

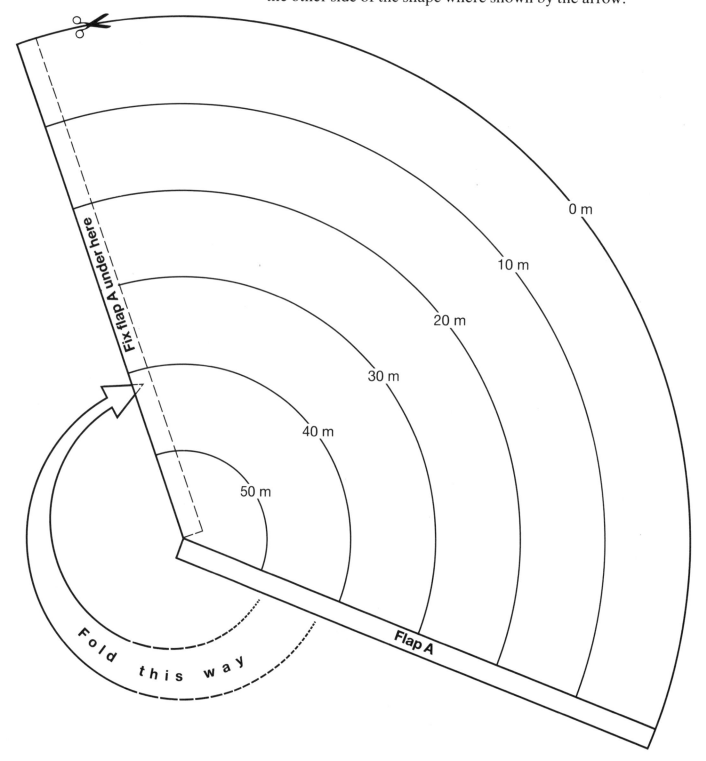

Make a hill

You have already seen that maps can show a variety of information. They can also show you how **high** the land is above the sea (**sea level**).

Join the numbered dots below. (A few have already been joined for you.)
● Join the dots numbered 0 with a **blue** line.
● Join the dots numbered 10 with a **light green** line.
● Using **light green**, shade the area between the blue line and the light green line.
● Join the dots numbered 20 with a **dark green** line.
● Using **dark green**, shade the area between the light green line and the dark green line.
● Join the dots numbered 30 with an **orange** line.
● Using **orange**, shade the area between the dark green line and the orange line.
● Join the dots numbered 40 with a **light brown** line.
● Using **light brown**, shade the area between the orange line and the light brown line.
● Using **dark brown**, shade the area inside the light brown line.

When you have drawn all the lines and completed the shading, do the following.
● Cut out the shape made by the **blue** line. Follow it right round.
● Place the shape on a piece of thick card. Draw carefully around it and then cut out the card to the **same shape.**
● Next cut out the slightly smaller shape made by the **light green** line. Place this shape on to another piece of thick card, trace carefully round it and then cut out the shape from the card as before. Fix this second piece of card on to the first in its **correct position**.
● Repeat by cutting out shapes along the **dark green** line, the **orange** line and the **light brown** line.
● Fix all the shapes together.

You have made a hill.

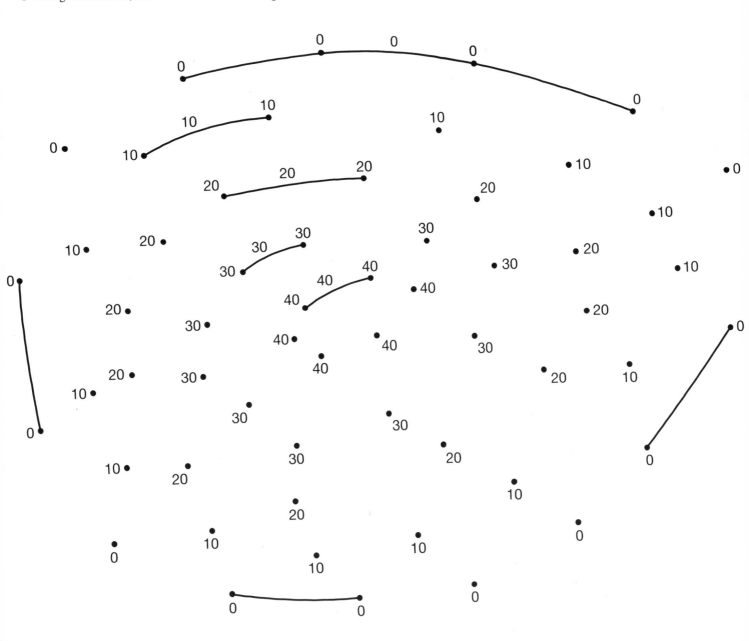

Siege

This is a game for two players.

One player is the Attacker and has an army of six divisions. Six tiddlywinks or paper counters which you make yourself stand for the six divisions. The other player is the Defender of the castle at the top of the hill.

How to play

● Each player makes his/her own spinner (see below left).
● All the divisions of the army begin at sea level, which is at **0 metres**.
● The Attacker tries to capture the castle. The Defender tries to destroy each of the Attacker's divisions.
● The Attacker spins first and moves one or more of the divisions up the hill by the number of metres shown on his/her spinner.
● The Defender spins second and may push back one of the Attacker's divisions by the number of metres shown on his/her spinner.
● When the Defender pushes a division back to sea level, that division is out of the game.
● If the Attacker succeeds in moving **two divisions** to the top of the hill at 60 m, the castle is captured and the Attacker has won the game.
● If the Defender succeeds in pushing **five divisions** back to sea level, the Attacker has been defeated and the Defender has won.

The Attacker's spinner

The Defender's spinner

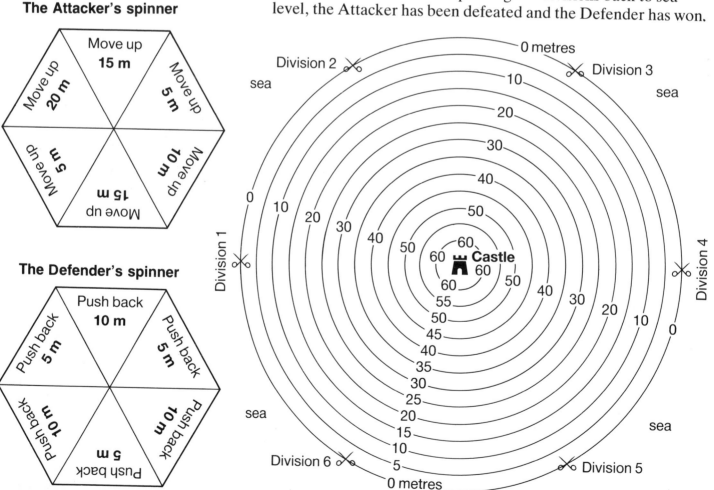

Join the dots

On the model you made on page 37, the outlines of the shapes are at different heights. But each of these outlines is **level** or **horizontal**.

Below are some more numbers to join. Use the following colours.
● Join the 0s with **blue**, the 10s with **light green**, the 20s with **dark green**, the 30s with **orange**, and the 40s with **light brown**.
● When you have drawn the lines in these colours, shade the areas between the lines as follows.

The area between 0 and 10	**light green**
The area between 10 and 20	**dark green**
The area between 20 and 30	**orange**
The area between 30 and 40	**light brown**
The area inside the 40 line	**dark brown**

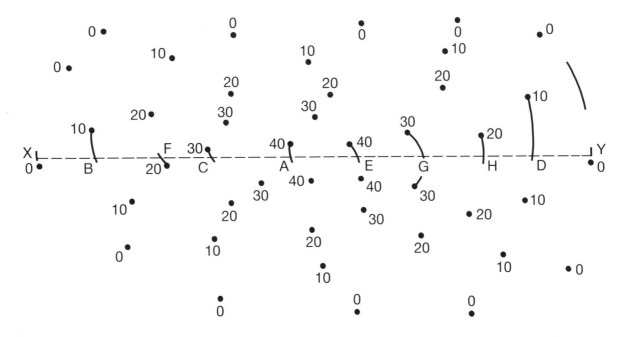

Each of the lines you have drawn shows a different **height** of the land **above sea level**. These are 0 m (which is at sea level), 10 m, 20 m, 30 m, 40 m. The land inside the 40 m line is higher than 40 m but does not reach 50 m.

Opposite are some columns of different heights.
● Shade the part of each column which is between 0 and 10 m **light green**.
● Shade the part of each column which is between 10 and 20 m **dark green**.
● Shade the part of each column which is between 20 and 30 m **orange**.
● Shade the part of each column which is between 30 and 40 m **light brown**.
● Cut out the columns. Stick them down on a piece of card. Cut out each column from the card. Fold each column along the dashed line to make a tab. Stick each column by its tab to

the map of lines you have completed above. Match the letters of the columns to those on the map. Make the columns **stand upright**.

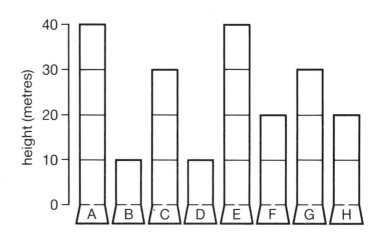

Make a cross-section

The dashed line marked X–Y on the map on page 39 is the same as the dashed line X–Y on the graph below. The graph also shows heights in metres.

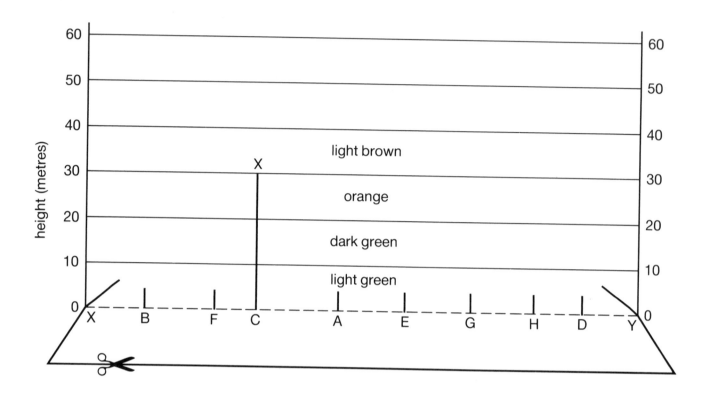

On the map on page 39, you fixed columns at points A, B, C, D, E, F, G and H. The position of the centre of each column is shown on the graph above.

The heights of the columns are **A** and **E**   **40** m
C and **G**   **30** m
F and **H**   **20** m
B and **D**   **10** m

What to do

● Draw each of the lines which have been started on the graph to their correct height. Line C has been drawn for you.
● Mark the top of each line with an ×.
● Join the × and shade in the area beneath the line in the colours shown on the graph.
● Join the top of line B to X at the left-hand end of the graph.
● Join the top of line D to Y at the right-hand end of the graph.
● Cut out carefully the shape you have shaded and stand it against the lines on your map on page 39.

You can now see what the shape of the hill is like when looked at from the side. This shape is called the **cross-section** of the hill.

● Stick the cross-section on the map to complete your model of the hill.

A map with contours

Contours tell us how high the land is. If you were to follow the line of a contour on a map when out for a walk, do you think you would follow a level course or go up and down?

_____

The map below shows some contours, a road and a river. Some other heights next to the dots have also been put on the map. These are called **spot heights**.

What to do

● Shade the road **red** and the river **blue**.
● Shade the land between 0 and 10 m at the southern edges of the map **light green**.
● Shade the land between 10 and 20 m **dark green**.
● Shade the land between 20 and 30 m **orange**.
● Shade the land between 30 and 40 m **light brown**.
● Shade the land above 40 m in the northern part of the map **dark brown**.
● Using the same colours, complete the key on the map.

Look at the map carefully then **circle** the correct answers below.

1 What is the height of the **highest** point on the map
   shown as a spot height?   30/40/43/50 m
2 What is the height of the **lowest** point on the map
   shown as a spot height?   0/5/10/20 m
3 What is the height of the bridge?   5/10/15/20/30 m
4 At what height does the road enter the
   map in the **west**?   10/15/20/25/30 m
5 At what height does the road leave the map
   in the **east**?   15/20/25/30/35 m
6 How much does the road **rise** between the bridge
   and the eastern edge of the map?   0/5/15/20/30 m
7 In which part of the map is the **highest** land
   to be found?   N/SE/NE/NW

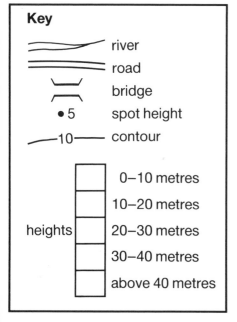

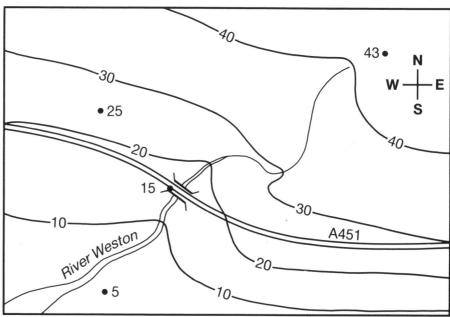

Westward Ho!

This is a game for two or three players.

The game is in three parts. These are: **The Voyage**, **Into the Interior** and **Land Grab Rummy**.

The Voyage

To play **The Voyage**, you will need the following:
- ☐ A die.
- ☐ A cardboard ship for each player. The ship is drawn at the bottom of the page. Cut it out and glue it to a piece of card. Each player should colour in his/her ship with a different colour.
- ☐ One copy of the map of the sea on page 43 and its key on page 44.
- ☐ A Log Book for each player. This is on page 44.
- ☐ A pen or pencil to write in the Log Book.

How to play

● You must sail your ship from East Balfour across the sea. You must go through one of the two gaps in the Barrier Reef. Then you must go to one of the three **safe landing places** on the new land. The key under the Log Book will help you to find these places. All your moves must take place on the map.

● The die shows the direction in which a ship should move.

If **1** or **2** is thrown, the player moves his/her ship **one square west**.

If **3** is thrown, the player moves his/her ship **one square north or south**.

If **4** is thrown, the player moves his/her ship **one square north-west or south-west**.

If **5** or **6** is thrown, the player can move his/her ship in **any direction** but by only **one square**.

● As the players move across the sea, they may have bad luck or good luck. They must look at the map and the key carefully. They must do what the key tells them when they land on squares which have a **sign** or **letter in them**.

● The players decide who throws the die first. Then all the players put their ships in square 8430. The first player throws the die and moves his/her ship **one square** in the direction shown on the die. The first player then fills in the **Log Book**. The other player or players then throw the die, move their ships and fill in their Log Books. The first player throws the die again, moves his/her ship and fills in the Log Book again. Play continues until each player reaches a safe **landing place**.

● Each player must land at a **different** landing place. This landing place will be the player's starting point for the next part of the game called **Into the Interior**. The first player to reach a safe landing place can claim **Bonus Points** which will be useful later. The first player can claim one Bonus Point for each extra throw of the die needed by his/her opponents to reach their safe landing places. The number of extra throws used can be seen in the opponents' Log Books. The Bonus Points are written on the **Claim Form** on page 48.

 Your ship

The map for The Voyage

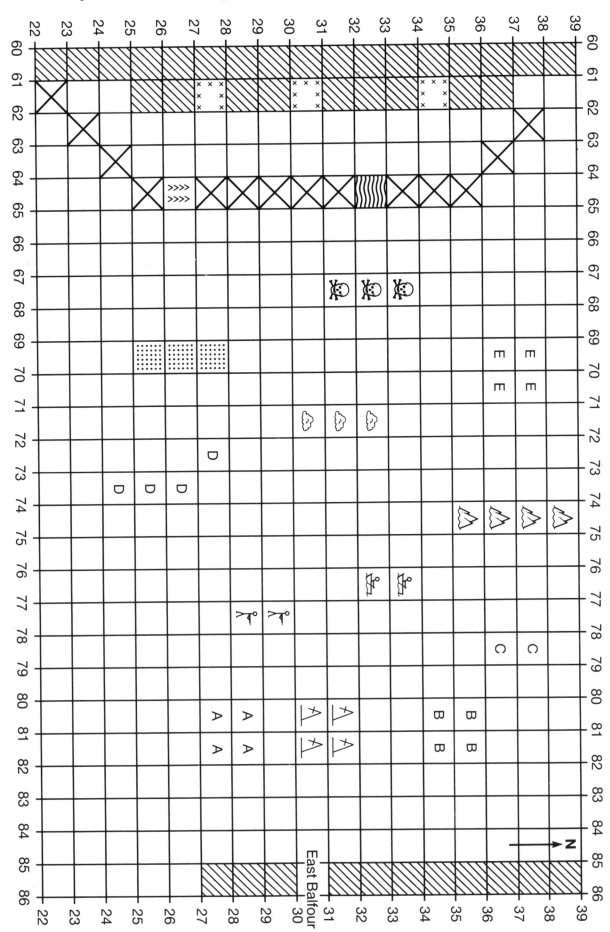

The Log Book for The Voyage

Every move you make across the sea from East Balfour to one of the safe landing places must be recorded in this Log Book. If you run out of space before reaching a safe landing place, ask your teacher for another Log Book page.

Move number	Number shown on die	Direction moved	Grid reference of square your ship has now moved to	Any events (see map and key)

The key for the map for The Voyage

Shallow channel. Miss a turn if your ship reaches this square.	Iceberg damage. Miss two turns.	A — Move to 7829
Deep channel. No problems.	Blown off course. Move to square 7128.	B — Move to 7936
Barrier reef. Your ship **cannot** move on to these squares.	Run aground on sand banks. Miss two turns.	C — Move to 7637
Broken mast. Miss a turn.	coastal area	D — Move to 7026
Mutiny. Miss two turns until order is restored.	safe landing place	E — Move to 6833
No wind. Miss a turn.	Pirates. Move eastwards. The number shown on the die is the number of squares you move.	

Into the Interior

The game continues with the same players.

To play **Into the Interior**, you will need the following.
- ☐ A spinner. The spinner is drawn below left. Cut it out carefully and glue it to cardboard. Carefully cut out the shape again and make a hole in the centre for a matchstick.
- ☐ A cardboard wagon for each player. The wagon is also drawn below. Cut it out and glue it to cardboard. You should colour your wagon the same as your ship.
- ☐ One copy of the map of the interior. This is drawn on page 46. A different coloured pencil for each player to mark his/her route.

How to play

- You must move your wagon from **your landing place** to one of the three **forts** shown on the map. The key at the bottom of this page will help you to find these places.
- You all spin in turn in the order in which you land. You start from **your own landing place** and move your wagon by doing what it says on the spinner.
- You can move in **any direction, but**

  When you reach a square with a **river** or **marsh** in it, you must **stop** in that square until you spin 'Cross a river or marsh'. You can then move **one** square.

  When you reach a square with a **contour** in it, you must **stop** in that square until you spin 'Move up 50 metres' or 'Move down 50 metres', depending upon which way you are going.

  The 'Move forward' parts of the spinner can only be used on squares which have nothing in them, or which look like this:

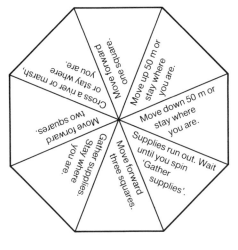

Your wagon

- Each player must reach a **different fort**. This fort will be the player's starting point for the last part of the game called **Land Grab Rummy**.
- The first player to reach a fort can claim **Bonus Points**, which will be useful later.
- That player can claim one Bonus Point for each extra spin of the spinner taken by his/her opponents to reach their forts. The Bonus Points are written on the **Claim Form** on page 48.

Key for map for Into the Interior and Land Grab Rummy

▨ coastal area	◡ river	⁙ fertile land which is easily farmed
⊠ safe landing place	50m contour line	♠ forest
⊎ marsh	⌂ fort	◇ land where minerals can be found

The maps for Into the Interior and Land Grab Rummy

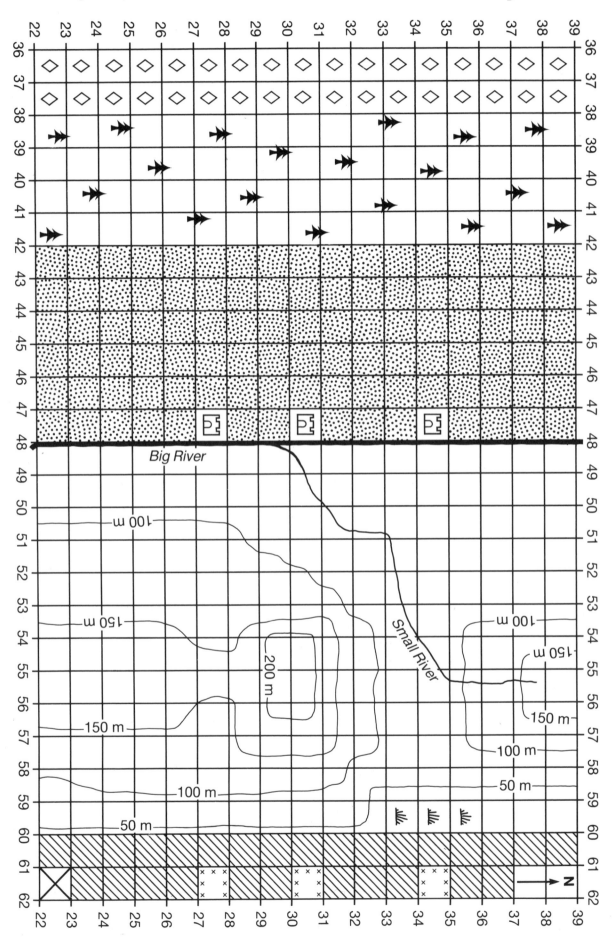

Land Grab Rummy

The game continues with the same players.

To play **Land Grab Rummy** you will need the following.
☐ A pack of playing cards.
☐ A Claim Form for each player (see page 48).
☐ One copy of the map on page 46.

How to play

● You have to claim land on the map. You can claim any of the land **west** of the Big River (grid line 48). The key at the bottom of page 45 will help you to see what the land can be used for.
● The pack of 52 playing cards show the types of land you can claim and the number of squares you can claim.
   Spades show **fertile land**, which can be easily farmed.
   Clubs show **forest**.
   Diamonds show **land where minerals can be found**.
   Hearts can be used to **claim land** from your opponents if it is **next to your own**.

These cards are worth

Ace to 10	one square of land each
Jack	two squares of land
Queen	three squares of land
King	four squares of land

● Also, a run of cards in a suit gains an **extra square** for each card in the run. For example, a run of 8, 9, 10 and Jack of Spades would be worth nine squares of fertile land. This is because the 8 equals one square, the 9 equals one square, the 10 equals one square, the Jack equals 2 squares, which add up to five squares. Add on one square for each of the cards 8, 9, 10 and the Jack, and the total is nine squares.

   A run must have at least three cards in it, and the cards must be of the same suit.

● The game is played in rounds. At the start of each round, the pack of cards is shuffled. The first player to reach a fort shuffles the pack for the first round and deals the cards. Players then take turns to shuffle and deal.

● The dealer deals 13 cards to each player. The remaining cards of the pack are put **face down** in the middle of the table.
● The dealer takes the top card from the pack. If he/she wants to keep this card, then he/she must put down **another** card, **face up** next to the pack.
● The second player can choose **either** the top card from the pack **or** the card which is face up. If he/she wants to keep either card, then he/she must put down **another** card, **face up** next to the pack.
● Each player must in turn choose a card and put one down. Players should **always have 13 cards in their hands**.

   The round continues until there are no cards left in the pack.

● When the round has ended, the players take turns to put any runs of cards on the table and claim land. The dealer starts first and the rest take turns to show each run and claim land. Only **Hearts** may be used to claim your **neighbour's land**. Hearts have the same value as other suits.
● When all the runs have been shown, single cards should then be shown. The single cards should be shown in turn one at a time to claim land. The dealer shows the first single card. Again, Hearts claim your neighbour's land.
● Players record their claims by doing the following. They must
   ☐ Put their initials in their squares.
   ☐ Fill in the grid references on the Claim Form.
   ☐ Fill in the Value Column of the Claim Form as follows:
      Fertile land equals 3 points a square.
      Forest equals 2 points a square.
      Land where minerals can be found equals 1 point a square.
● Play continues until all the squares of land have been claimed.
● If you lose land, you must rub out your initials on the map and the grid references of these squares on the Claim Form. You must also change the Value Column.
● The winner of Land Grab Rummy is the player who has the highest score in the Value Column.

Claim Form for Land Grab Rummy

The grid references of squares claimed are recorded on this form.

● In the top box, write the value of your Bonus Points from **The Voyage**.

● In the other box, write the value of your Bonus Points from **Into the Interior**.

● If you run out of space before the game has ended, ask your teacher for another page like this one.

Bonus Points from **The Voyage**	
Bonus Points from **Into the Interior**	

Round number	Grid reference of squares claimed	Value of each square
1		
2		
3		
4		
5		
6		
7		
8		
9		
10		
11		
12		
13		
14		
15		
16		
17		
18		
19		
20		
21		
22		
23		
24		
25		
26		
27		
28		
29		
30		

Total value